WRESTLING SUPERST★RS

DOLPH ZIGGLER

BY JESSE ARMSTRONG

EPIC

BELLWETHER MEDIA • MINNEAPOLIS, MN

EPIC BOOKS are no ordinary books. They burst with intense action, high-speed heroics, and shadows of the unknown. Are you ready for an Epic adventure?

This edition first published in 2015 by Bellwether Media, Inc.

No part of this publication may be reproduced in whole or in part without written permission of the publisher. For information regarding permission, write to Bellwether Media, Inc., Attention: Permissions Department, 5357 Penn Avenue South, Minneapolis, MN 55419.

Library of Congress Cataloging-in-Publication Data

Armstrong, Jesse.
  Dolph Ziggler / by Jesse Armstrong.
    pages cm. – (Epic. Wrestling Superstars)
  Includes bibliographical references and index.
  Summary: "Engaging images accompany information about Dolph Ziggler. The combination of high-interest subject matter and light text is intended for students in grades 2 through 7"– Provided by publisher.
  Audience: Age: 7-12.
  ISBN 978-1-62617-179-4 (hardcover : alk. paper)
  1. Ziggler, Dolph, 1980–Juvenile literature. 2. Wrestlers–United States–Biography–Juvenile literature. I. Title.
  GV1196.Z54.A75 2015
  796.812092–dc23
  [B]
                    2014040190

Printed in the United States of America, North Mankato, MN.

TABLE OF CONTENTS

WARNING!

The wrestling moves used in this book are performed by professionals.
Do not attempt to reenact any of the moves performed in this book.

THE DEBUT

Dolph Ziggler struts to the ring for his **debut**. He introduces himself to fans. Then he extends his hand to Batista. But his handshake turns into a slap.

BATISTA

Ziggler slips through the ropes a few
times. Then he and Batista exchange blows.
A Batista Bomb puts Ziggler down for good.
He loses the match but shows his talent.

WHO IS DOLPH ZIGGLER?

Dolph Ziggler is a **showoff** in the WWE ring. The superstar with bleached-blond hair makes sure opponents and fans notice him. He is proud of his skills.

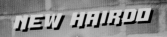

NEW HAIRDO

★

Ziggler cut his hair short and dyed it dark once. He disliked the new look.

LIFE
BEFORE
WWE

Ziggler was a star wrestler as an amateur.
He competed in high school and college.
He set records at both levels.

In college, Ziggler studied **political science**. He planned to go to law school until WWE drafted him.

ALWAYS
THE PERFORMER

★

Ziggler has also tried stand-up
comedy. He enjoys any
chance to be in front of
an audience.

A WWE SUPERSTAR

FIRST LOOK

★

Ziggler dressed as a golf caddy when he went by Nick Nemeth.

STAR PROFILE

WRESTLING NAME: Dolph Ziggler

REAL NAME: Nicholas Theodore Nemeth

BIRTHDATE: July 27, 1980

HOMETOWN: Cleveland, Ohio

HEIGHT: 6 feet (1.8 meters)

WEIGHT: 213 pounds (97 kilograms)

WWE DEBUT: 2008 (as Dolph Ziggler)

FINISHING MOVE: Zig Zag

WWE offered Ziggler a developmental contract in 2004. In 2005, he wrestled as Nick Nemeth. Then he was a male cheerleader with the Spirit Squad.

In 2008, Ziggler became a **heel** named Dolph.
Fans did not cheer him on. Still, he rose to the
top and has been a champion many times.

WINNING MOVES

The Zig Zag is Ziggler's finishing move.
He leaps at an opponent from behind. Then
he grabs him by the head and falls backward.

ZIG ZAG

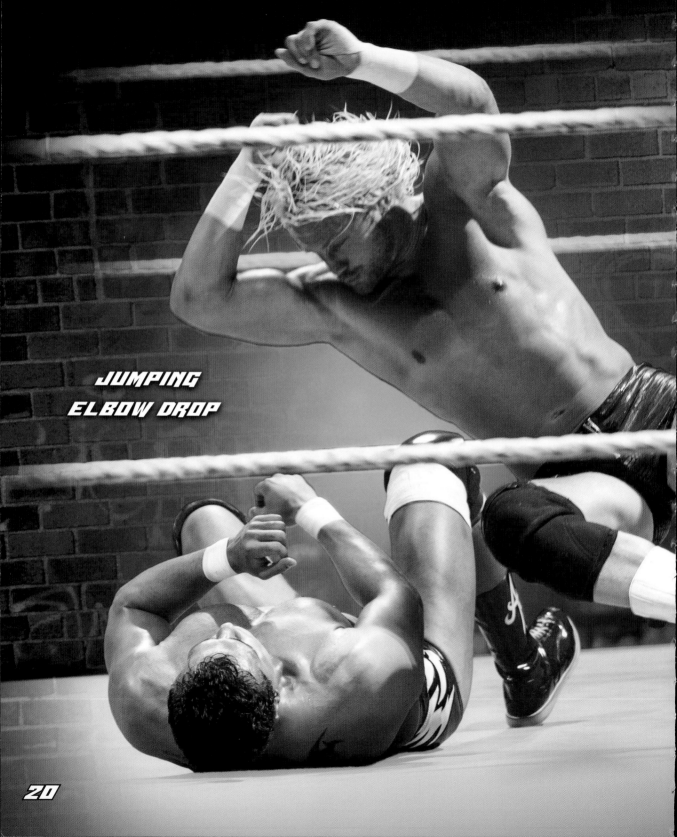

JUMPING
ELBOW DROP

Ziggler uses a variety of other **signature moves**, too. One is the Jumping Elbow Drop. He jumps into the air and elbows his opponent on the ground. Ouch!

GLOSSARY

amateur—not a professional; athletes who are amateurs are not paid and participate in sports for fun.

debut—first official appearance

developmental contract—an agreement between WWE and a wrestler; WWE promises to train the wrestler in smaller leagues.

drafted—to be selected for a team or group

finishing move—a wrestling move that finishes off an opponent

heel—a wrestler viewed as a villain

political science—the study of government and laws

showoff—a person who likes to be the center of attention

signature moves—moves that a wrestler is famous for performing

TO LEARN MORE

At the Library

Armstrong, Jesse. *Kofi Kingston*. Minneapolis, Minn.:
Bellwether Media, 2015.

Black, Jake. *WWE General Manager's Handbook*. New York,
N.Y.: Grosset & Dunlap, 2012.

West, Tracey. *Race to the Rumble*. New York, N.Y.: Grosset &
Dunlap, 2011.

On the Web

Learning more about Dolph Ziggler
is as easy as 1, 2, 3.

1. Go to www.factsurfer.com.

2. Enter "Dolph Ziggler" into the search box.

3. Click the "Surf" button and you will see a list
of related web sites.

With factsurfer.com, finding more information
is just a click away.

INDEX